(c) 2017 Sophia Lorraine

All rights reserved.

ISBN-13: 978-1-945887-43-7

ISBN-10: 1-945887-43-5

Every effort has been made to ensure that the information in this book was correct at press time. The author and publisher disclaim liability to any party for any loss, damage, or disruption caused by errors or omissions, whether such errors or omissions result from negligence, accident, or any other cause.

Visit us at gumdroppress.com

Bana Alabed was born June 7, 2009. She lived peacefully in Aleppo, Syria, for the first three years of her life.

But then fighting broke out in her city between the Syrian government and the rebel groups that opposed it.

When she was 7 years old, and with the help of her mother Fatemah, Band Started tweeting to the world.

Her message was simple: She wanted the world to stand with Aleppo, to help stop the bombing of her city.

She said, "I just want to live without fear" and explained that she wrote "to forget" the bombings."

Two months later, her family's home was destroyed in the bombing. Bana was sad, writing, "My beloved dolls died in the bombing".

Bana's school was destroyed, too, but author J. K. Rowling sent her an ebook from the Harry Potter series so she could read that.

Band tried not to let her spirit be broken. She said, "No one knows my life is difficult when I smile."

In December 2016, the Syrian government recaptured the city of Aleppo. Bana and her family, including her little brother, were evacuated from Aleppo to Turkey.

Even after Bana was safe in Turkey, she continued to speak for her people, saying, "Let's now join together for peace across Syria."

She and her mom became citizens of Turkey in May 2017. Bana still loved her city and tweeted using the hashtag #AleppoIsInMyHeart.

Bana celebrated her 8th birthday from the safety of her new home in Turkey.

She was able to return to school and pursue her education. Bana wants to be an author and a teacher.

In October 2017, Bana published a book called "DEAR WORLD" sharing her experiences and calling for world peace.

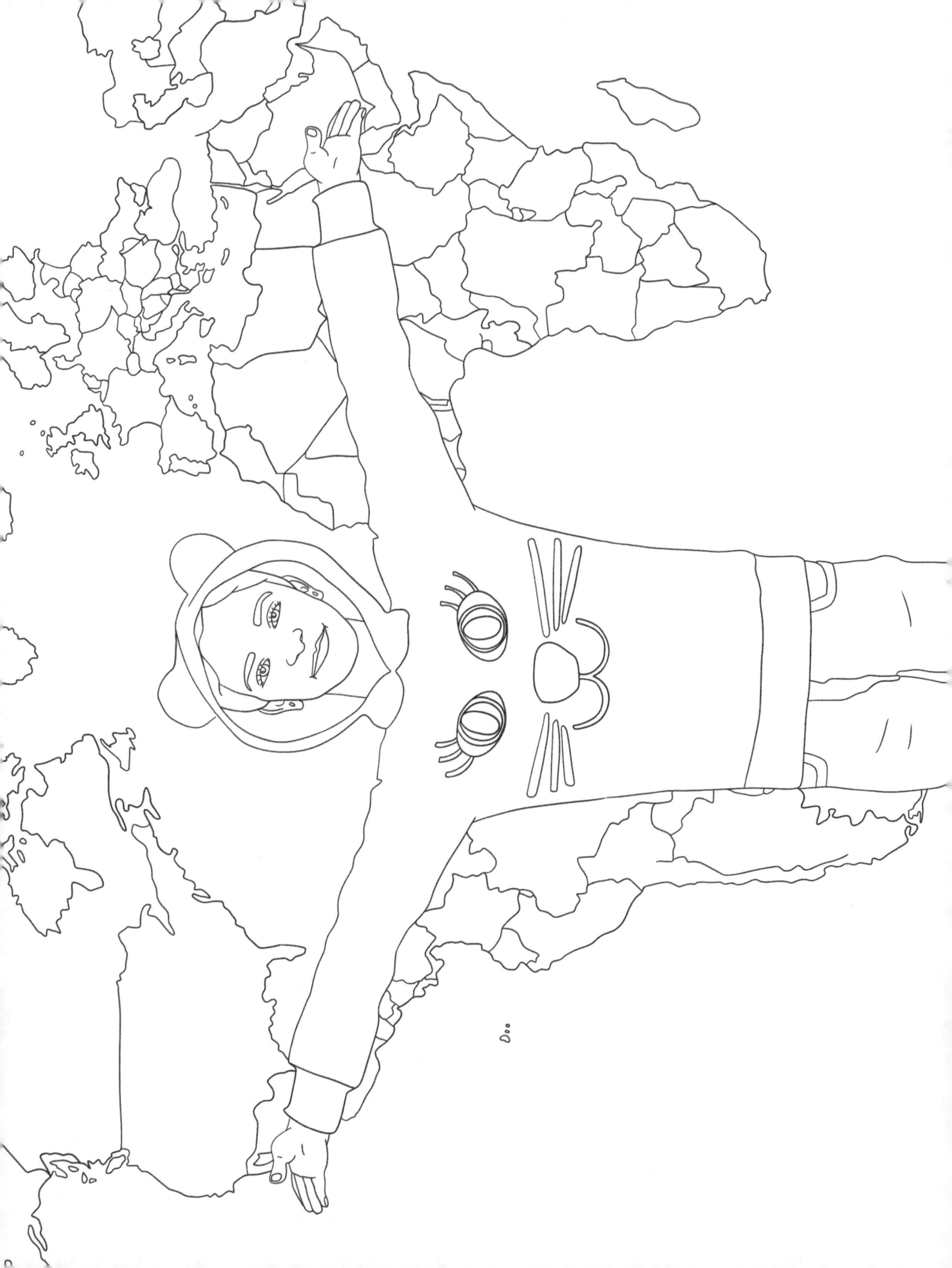

As Bana explained, "I am a child with something to say," and that's let's and help every child in [a] war zone."

www.ingramcontent.com/pod-product-compliance
Lightning Source LLC
Chambersburg PA
CBHW081356080526
44588CB00016B/2509